NATURAL LIGHT

Portraits of Scottish Writers
Angela Catlin

Introduction by Trevor Royle

PAUL HARRIS PUBLISHING / WATERFRONT

III

First published in Great Britain in 1985
by Paul Harris Publishing/Waterfront,
Leith, Edinburgh

Photographs copyright © Angela Catlin 1985
Introduction copyright © Trevor Royle 1985
Text copyright © Contributors 1985

ISBN cased 0 86228 101 6
limp 0 86228 102 4

The publishers gratefully acknowledge
The Scottish Arts Council for financial assistance in
publication of this volume.

Printed in Great Britain by Netherwood Dalton & Co Ltd
Typeset by Witwell Limited, Liverpool
Designed by Charles Miller Graphics, Edinburgh

British Library Cataloguing in Publication Data
Catlin, Angela
    Natural light : portraits of Scottish writers.
1. Photography—Portraits
2. Authors, Scottish—20th Century—Portraits
I. Title
779′.2′0924   TR681.A5

ISBN 0-86228-101-6
ISBN 0-86228-102-4 Pbk

NATURAL LIGHT

I

Photographer's note

The people in this book represent a wide cross-section of contemporary Scottish writers. Shooting and compiling this series of photographs entailed extensive travel over most of the British Isles and, reflecting upon the portraits presented here, I believe the results to have been worthwhile.

II

NATURAL LIGHT

Portraits of Scottish Writers
Angela Catlin

Contents

V

VI

INTRODUCTION

Amongst the holdings in the substantial photographic archive maintained by Edinburgh Public Libraries there is a Hill-Adamson calotype of Professor John Wilson, the irascible editor and author who flourished in the first half of the nineteenth century, writing under the pen-name of 'Christopher North'. It was taken in 1844 and seeing it for the first time is akin to the sensation one would presumably experience on being told that Bonnie Prince Charlie or Robert Burns were still in the land of the living, so powerful is the sheer historical presence of the man. Wilson's leonine features, his red, flaming locks and his large frame have been well enough described by contemporaries and friends like Thomas Carlyle and John Gibson Lockhart, but the photographic evidence provided by the calotype is immediate and arresting. Then in his fifty-ninth year, there is still confirmation a-plenty of the burly athlete who won fame at Oxford for his ability to leap great distances, and who, in his youth, tramped the length and breadth of Britain and Ireland. He sits there, four-square to the world, his eyes darkening beneath bristling brows, an arm slung elegantly over the side of his chair, a wine glass within easy reach, the very epitome of a man of letters. Today, Christopher North is remembered best for his scurrilous attacks on literary and political enemies in the pages of *Blackwood's Magazine* and for his comic ruse in guying the great and good in the Chaldee Manuscript of 1817: his novels and poetry, fashionable in their day, have long ago been condemned to Time's wastepaper basket. But in the calotype he comes alive again; it is still possible to feel in its sepia tones and in Wilson's mannered pose something of the energy which vibrated through this extraordinary, dangerous, though quirkily gifted man.

When Wilson's friend and one-time literary collaborator, John Gibson Lockhart, first came across this revolutionary photographic technique he remarked that the calotype, as invented by David Octavius Hill and Robert Adamson 'is about to revolutionise book illustration entirely'. Significantly, he added the thought that the new method should also be considered as an art form of the highest order. Of his two prophecies the first had come true by the end of the century; the second has only come to be accepted in fairly recent times. Photography did change the face of book production, allowing the reader to have both literary and artistic evidence about any subject under discussion and most non-fiction books became more lively as a result. In that sense, the record provided by the well-tempered photograph was another turn in the wheel of progress, but as they became more professional in their execution, so too did many photographs

7

begin to lose their artistic appeal. Publishers — and authors — started to use them as a means to an end with scant regard being paid to the artistic energy involved in their creation. It is only of late that we have come to realise that the photograph, especially the photographic portrait, can be as telling in its execution as the portrait in oils. A mere glance at the work of photographers like Jane Bown, Karsh of Ottawa or Don McCullin confirms the truth that beyond the artifice of lens, film, paper and chemicals lies the eye of an artist.

When Hill and Adamson asked Wilson to sit for them — Lord Cockburn was another literary model — they were dong little more than exploiting a medium they had invented for making pictures. In other words, they grasped at an early stage the artistic possibilities inherent in the calotype, and from the evidence of their output, I suspect, too, that their vision was shared by the sitters. They were not to know that by the end of the century portrait photography, debased by commercialism, was to transform itself into stilted and stiff family groups or the impersonal mug-shot. The widespread ownership of modern cameras gave immortality of a kind to the family group or to the holiday snap which, however amateur or pedestrian the execution, were things of beauty in the eye of the fond beholder. Similarly, professional portrait photography became as meaningless and boring as the boardroom portrait: most writers today are only photographed because their publishers require a publicity snap for the fly-leaf of a book's dust-jacket.

It is, though, still possible to take a mechanical box and to produce results which are memorable enough to embed themselves in the memory, in much the same way that a good painting will excite the upper brain cells. This is the mystery at the heart of photography all practitioners of the art attempt to discover. To achieve that aim requires skill and patience as well as technical ability. Above all, it requires humanity, for the camera is an impersonal instrument like the writer's typewriter or the painter's brush; an essential tool which imposes a barrier between its operator and the sitter. The successful photographer is the patient artist who overcomes that barrier to capture a moment of truth: that, it seems to me, is what Angela Catlin achieved by the time she had completed her project to photograph a group of Scottish writers.

During the spring and summer of 1984 she set out on a personal odyssey to record forty-nine authors in a series of photographic portraits. There was no sense of literary competition in her choice; rather they are a selection of writers of Scots birth, or to use Muriel Spark's phrase, 'of Scots formation', either living in Scotland or elsewhere in the United Kingdom. (Some writers declined Angela Catlin's invitation, others were unavailable or out of the country at the time.) Each was photographed at home or in a setting which appealed both to photographer and her subject and which allowed her to stalk her prey. Her method was deceptively simple. There was no unnecessary foreplay with banks of arc lights or nervous checks with light meters: natural light and a sound eye were enough. Then, when the sitter was talking, or unprepared, or sitting in repose, Angela Catlin chose the moment of consummation. The results are singularly impressive — a series of portraits which captures each writer in a new and sometimes quite unexpected light.

The camera cannot disclose any inner truths about a writer's work; neither should a casual glance or the set of an arm be taken as evidence of any literary insight. In that sense, the camera is not a magical box capable of revealing the secrets of literary creation. And yet, after viewing Angela Catlin's suite of portraits, each of the sitters seemed to appear to me in a different guise. All of them I have known for a number of years, some as intimate friends, others as casual acquaintances. Each face is as familiar to me as many others I meet in the daily round. But seeing them through Angela Catlin's eyes provided me — and I hope will provide others — with the sensation of seeing them as if for the first time. To take two examples: Norman MacCaig, caught in the half light of his living room, is redolent of the voice I hear in his poem 'A Man in My Position' and seeing George Bruce's stark portrait reminded me that he comes from the north-east, 'In rock land and salt pasture/To the round of sea. Nothing more.' Others, too, will have their own discoveries to make in the shape and texture of Angela Catlin's portraits.

Sir Walter Scott was fond of joking that his portrait had been painted so many times at Abbotsford that eventually Maida, his old deer hound and constant romantic accessory in such ploys, would angrily leave the room at the first sight of a painter unpacking easel and colour box. No such fear chills the hounds of Scotland's writers today. With a few honourable exceptions — one remembers with gratitude Alexander Moffatt's masterly paintings and Jessie Ann Matthew's accompanying photographs for the 'Seven Poets' exhibition of 1981 (MacDiarmid, MacCaig, Crichton Smith, Mackay Brown, Garioch, MacLean, Morgan) — few writers have been captured in contemporary portraiture. Angela Catlin's record is therefore all the more welcome. When she set out very few of the writers were known to her personally: by the end of her assignment and with the publication of the book it is possible to see just how intimate and truthful is the relationship between photographer and sitter, between artist and writer.

All of the writers agreed to provide a sample of their writing to accompany their photograph — work in progress, a favourite piece of writing, an autobiographical sketch — but the book is Angela Catlin's alone. Her eye made it. No one but she could have seen the writers in this particular way, in this natural light.

Trevor Royle
December 1984

9

Hamish Henderson

NINTH ELEGY

Fort Capuzzo

For there will come a day
when the Lord will say
– Close Order!

One evening, breaking a jeep journey at Capuzzo
I noticed a soldier as he entered the cemetery
and stood looking at the grave of a fallen enemy.
Then I understood the meaning of the hard word 'pietas'
(a word unfamiliar to the newsreel commentator
as well as to the pimp, the informer and the traitor).

He thought was like this. — Here's another 'Good Jerry'!
Poor mucker. Just eighteen. Must be hard-up for man-power.
Or else he volunteered, silly bastard. That's the fatal.
the — fatal — mistake. Never volunteer for nothing.
I wonder how he died? Just as well it was him, though,
and not one our chaps. ... Yes, the only good Jerry,
as they say, is your sort, chum.
            Cheerio, you poor bastard.
Don't be late on parade when the Lord calls 'Close order'.
Keep waiting for the angels. Keep listening for Reveille.

Alan Spence

6 HAIKU

the flowering plant nods
acknowledging
my gaze

using a peach
for a paperweight;
summer breeze

chained to its post
the guard-dog barks
at the pouring rain

the cold wind
rattles the bones
of the scarecrow

after the fireworks,
cold and still,
the moon

the snowman
calmly awaiting
the thaw

James Allan Ford

from *THE DUNCAN FLAW*

The winter sun, distant as it was, still reached the Sunday spires and steeples of Morningside, touching them with feeble gilt, lifting the eyes. I to the hills. He rejoiced in the surge of power as he accelerated to take the rise of Comiston Road towards Fairmilehead, the city boundary, the house at Whinbrae. From whence doth come mine aid. Then he glimpsed a pot-hole too late to avoid it and heard a clattering of exhaust pipe that made him take the Lord's name in vain. As suddenly downcast as he had been suddenly elated, he drew in to the kerb. He was going to be late again at Whinbrae, and Danny was a stickler for punctuality, a woman in a winged chariot. But how could a man keep to time, the way the world was? — a pot-hole in a main road within the city limits, where even a tardy rate-payer had a right to expect an unbroken surface; an exhaust assembly apparently designed to break loose at a shrug of the driver's shoulders; a minor repair that none of the nearby garages was likely to tackle on a day made sacred to idleness or double-time. Gripping the steering-wheel as if he were gripping the throats of all road-menders, exhaust-makers, car-repairers and other enemies of the realm, he swore in soldierly style. Then, with an old soldier's resourcefulness, a bachelor's independence, he took a piece of string from the glove compartment and a plastic sheet from the boot and, lying on his back, secured the exhaust pipe to its broken bracket. It was a cold road to lie on. His buttocks felt chilled, his anus tight. *Anus?* B'God, yes, the Roman word was the right one this time — a tighter word than the Anglo-Saxon *arsehole*. Thus spake Andrew Duncan, Major, M.C., last of the orthographic printers.

To complete the repairs to himself, he turned off the main road and drove to the Braid Hills Hotel, where he washed his hands and bought a large whisky. At the bar he met Walter Skene, moodily replenishing his beer-mug to maintain the swell of his belly.

"You'll join us?" Walter nodded glumly towards a table where his wife and daughter-in-law sat with empty glasses and vacant expressions.

"Not today, thanks. I've a pastoral visit to make, d'you see?" He had already brought Peter and Jenny to life for the day. He had Danny waiting to be wakened to joy. He could not make a profession out of lifting other people's eyes to the hills. But, with his glass in his hand, he followed Walter to the Skene table to offer token civility.

Walter himself was not in participating mood, his fleshy bulk seeming almost uninhabited. But his ladies were ready for communion and nourished the newcomer with happy attention. They were all well, he was assured, except of course Walter's son, who had stayed at home with his peptic ulcer. *Peptic*, Andrew reflected, was far too cheerful a word to associate with any ailment of Jamie Skene's.

Ron Butlin

DESCRIPTIONS OF THE FALLING SNOW

I described a flight of imaginary birds
across an imaginary sky in words
that played out every laboured game of skill
involving consonants and vowels, until
sufficient universal truths obeyed
the cadences of my trade.

I argued love and metaphysics through
by sound, resolving dissonance into
a line of formal spontaneity:
a passionate description of, let's say,
the falling snow. These were not dreams
but calculations for what seems

a well-constructed winter-sky. Neatly
stammered syllables of discreetly
quantified despair described the view:
some fields of hardened grass and mud; a few
abandoned tractors; a waterfall's cascade
stiffening into ice. I made

events from over twenty years ago
translate into each metaphor — as though
a door slammed shut, or someone's name
had set the limits to my suffering.
(And if the phrase read awkwardly I'd pause,
checking each effect for flaws).

The qualities of light through falling snow;
the patterns made by frost; the fields below
my house — I scanned and stressed a thousand words
describing everything I saw. The birds
in flight across the imaginary skies
sang what I set down — my lies

were coming true. And yet, I cannot live
uncorrupted by the narrative
I tell. All things are mine to name:
there is no innocence, no shame;
nothing is, that is not of my own
and of my incantation.

My fingers claw at imaginary birds.
My tongue stutters over lists of words
I've learnt by heart. Such passionate pretence!
It is almost five o'clock. I sense
the hammer strike the bell and cancel-out
each pitiless belief and doubt.

Alexander Scott

ISN'T IT SEMANTIC?

("Glasgow's Miles Better." — Glasgow City Chambers slogan.)
Glasgow's Males Batter.
Glasgow's Smile 's Bitter.

Douglas Dunn

AUBADE

A warm blue deity has given a summer say-so
To his (or her) creation of swifts and swallows.

It is a principle of Early to be still,
Counting the morning's numbers in the parish bell —

A yawn, a kiss, a noticing of light, a pause,
Watching the northlight touch household auroras.

Iain Crichton Smith

THE SOLDIER AND THE LAUGHING GIRL
by VERMEER

The soldier sits at the table
masterful in his red and black.

On one wall there is a map.

The window is open wide.

Directly opposite
a girl listens to his tale
of victory in battle.

His large black ribboned hat
is cocked at a rakish slant
Regard her pure warm smile
as if her very soul
had surrendered to his light
legendary story.
What pathos and delight,
alive and transitory!

Lavinia Derwent

THE KIRK MOOSE

I'm a wee kirk moose an' I haven't got a name,
But thon muckle kirk at the corner is ma hame,
Wi' the cock on the steeple an' the bells that gang "Ding!",
An' I wush that I was big enough to gaur them gie a ring.

I can sing a' the psalms, I can say a' the prayers,
An' I whiles do a dance up an' doon the pulpit stairs.
I ken a' the texts, I can find them in the Book,
An' there's mony a human bein' wi' nae notion whaur to look.

When the meenister says "Firstly" an' the folk a' settle doon,
I gang creepin'-creepin'-creepin' in amang their Sunday shoon,
An' I'm hopin', as I'm jinkin' frae the passage to the pew,
That they'll mebbe drap a jujube or a peppermint to chew.

For I'm sometimes awfu hungry, an' there's naethin' much to eat,
Except the Par-a-phrases or a hymn buik for a treat.
I've eaten the Auld Hunner, I've chowed Beatitudes,
But I canna say I've found them just the tastiest o' foods.

I'm a wee kirk moose an' I haven't got a name,
But I'm really quite contented. It's just ma empty waim.
So I'm hopin' that some Sunday, wad ye mind aboot me, please,
An' bring me in your Bibles just a wee bit dad o' cheese?

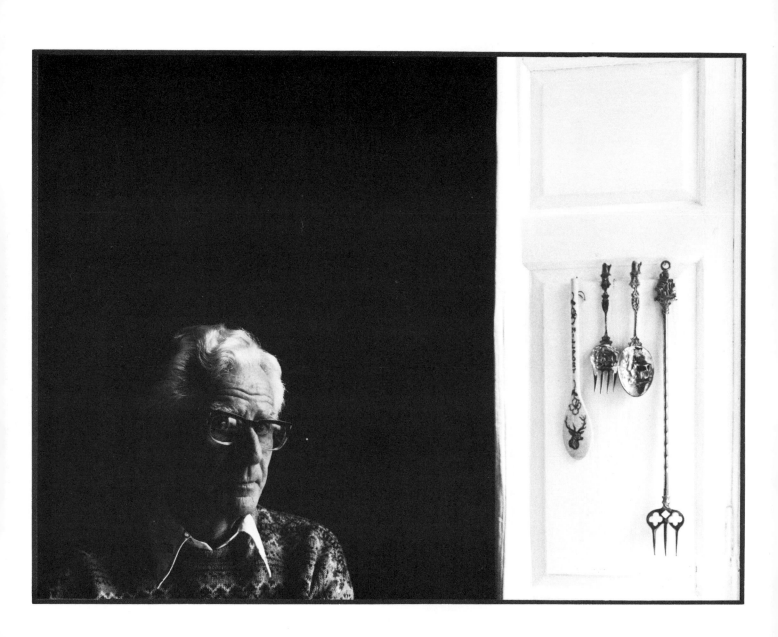

Robin Jenkins

from *POVERTY CASTLE*

He had always hoped that in his old age he would be able to write a novel that would be a celebration of goodness, without any need of irony. The characters in it would be happy because they deserved to be happy. It must not shirk the ills that flesh was heir to nor shut its eyes to the horrors of his century, the bloodiest in the history of mankind. It would have to triumph over these and yet speak the truth. Since he would wish also to celebrate the beauty of the earth he would set his story in his native Highlands, close to the sea.

In his 73rd year, when his powers were beginning to fail, he realised it was then or never. From the point of view of the world's condition the time would never be propitious. Fears of nuclear holocausts increased. Millions guzzled while millions starved. Everywhere truth was defiled, authority abused. Those shadows darkened every thinking person's mind: he could not escape them. They would make it hard for his novel to succeed.

"Impossible, I would say," said his wife, Jessie, a frank and cheerful Glaswegian. "You've always been severe on your characters, Donald. I can't see you changing now."

They were sitting in deck chairs on the grassy patch — it was too rough and sheep-trodden to be called a lawn — in front of their cottage overlooking the Firth of Clyde, about fifteen miles from the Holy Loch. It was a warm summer afternoon. Red Admiral butterflies fluttered in flocks from one buddleia bush to another. From the safety of rhododendrons chaffinches mocked Harvey the white cat asleep in the shade. Making for the opening to the sea, between the Wee Cumbrae and Bute, slunk an American submarine, black and sinister, laden with missiles.

In his childhood, in the West Highland village of Kilmory, there had been black beetles of repulsive appearance to which he and his friends had attributed deadly powers. Whenever one was encountered everybody had to spit with revulsion and yet also with a kind of terrified reverence, to ward off its mysterious evil. When he had grown up he had learned that the creatures were harmless, but he remembered them whenever he saw one of those submarines.

Walter Perrie

SONNET: TO YOU AND I, DEAR

To you and I, dear, in our shuttered room
the drumming seems by distance muted:
marches and motley, the public doom
in appropriate poses, unsuited
to nakedness. Let the password here
be *defencelessness* and bodies act
their own adventures, our sole frontier
be fantasy, our only law, their pact.
But through the whispered *please* or *dear*
the drums intrude, insistent, near,
subsuming love's irregular beat
in unisons of marching feèt
for private loves shall troop and turn
in worlds where other passions burn.

Archie Hind

from *THE DEAR GREEN PLACE*

He was standing on the bridge looking over the parapet into the dirty water, at the very spot where Boswell had stood and looked at the widest streets in the whole of Europe. Gles Chu! Glasgow! The dear green place! Now a vehicular sclerosis, a congestion of activity! He felt for a cigarette in his pocket and the match which he lit flared bitterly in the cold air. The city about him seemed so real, the buildings, the bridge, the trams, the buses, so separate and hard and discrete and other. He felt again a wave of nostalgia for another kind of existence — waxed fruit, sword sticks, snuff, tobacco, shining brass valves, steam pipes, jet ware, wag-at-the-wa's, horse-hair sofas, golf cleeks, cahootchie balls — all the symbols of confidence, possibility, energy, which had lived before this knotted, tight, seized-up reality which was around him had come to be.

He looked over towards where the obelisk in the park squatted, obscene. With its memories, Omdurman, Ypres, Tel-el-Kebir, screaming pipes, whisky, sweeping moustaches, regimental dinners, photographs in barbers' shops and boys with malacca canes. Brass button sticks and old medals in junk shops. The park looked grey like a plucked fowl with its stark leafless trees. He leaned on the smooth granite parapet of the bridge easing the weight on his legs. Glasgow! Gles Chu! The dear green place!

David Black

THE HANDS OF FELICITY

And now those
oxen haul in a ring! The mighty stones they
grind together are squeezing from my brain this
juice of poetry; it renews itself and
must not shrivel or flood, but daily
build up, and, by the oxen's exertions, empty . . .
It is therefore my skull submits to this con-
trition; therefore each day the discipline is
reimposed on the stalwart, slothful oxen;
therefore too, though one calls it second-best, the
will stays tight in the saddle and gives orders.
And perhaps in the end we'll have less need of
that!

Dorothy Dunnett

I sometimes think I only write books because I love travelling so much. I've been to Turkey, Russia and all the places I talk about, although I do read up the place first. My total reading list for the Lymond books was about six hundred by the end, and for Macbeth it was worse. It's just as well that I do go to the spot, because everyone checks up on me. I get messages from holidaymakers in Malta, asking to see the books I got out of the Royal Library at Valetta, and someone wrote from Blois saying she thought the Town Clerk ought to be approached to put up a map of the Rooftop Race. It's only on the spot, anyway, that I can get the final books and maps I read. A beautiful sixteenth century map in Lyons, showing every street and every house in the city was the basis for Lymond's and Philippa's movements in *Checkmate*, and I used two maps bought from the Left Bank in Paris to plot the action round the Rue de la Cerisee.

With *King Hereafter* it was even more important, for the vital books on Breton and Norman history were more readily found in St Malo and Coutances than in the British Library and the Widener Library at Harvard University in America proved a better source for information about Iona (it has a huge Celtic collection, and I had access to the stacks) than the National Library of Scotland, with its index limitations and the forms to fill in. Foreign Museums are also extremely important for what they show of clothes and fabrics, weapons, books and jewels. I was nearly arrested in the Treasure House at Topkapi in Istanbul, I spent so long there with my notebook. I take photographs, too, and when every detail really matters (as when plotting a murder on the golf course in the Bahamas) I sometimes mutter into a tape recorder. The only unhelpful library authorities I've ever found were in Moscow, where I wrote well in advance to the Director of Archives, on the advice of the National Library, but without obtaining a response. Contacted by telephone through an interpretor, on arrival in Russia, the Archives department blandly remarked that nothing could be done, as I should have sent an official government request, plus an offer on paper from the National Library to supply equivalent search and photocopying facilities to a Russian researcher ... In vain I pointed out that in Scotland such facilities were automatically already available to a bona fide researcher, but no dice.

Fred Urquhart

from *MISS HOGG AND MISS CAIRNS*

"When you go to the supermarket on Saturday," Mrs Hogg said, "don't forget to get one of those Bakewell tarts."

"I won't be going to the supermarket on Saturday," her daughter said. "You know perfectly well, Mother, I never go to the supermarket on Saturdays. I haven't been near the supermarket on a Saturday for years."

"Oh no, of course, it's your golfing day," Mrs Hogg said. "I can't see why you have to spend your entire Saturday playing golf. I've told you often enough, and I'll tell you again, Babbie Hogg, golfing is not a suitable game for a woman."

"And I've told you often enough, Mother, that I don't spend the entire Saturday playing golf," Miss Hogg said. "I only play golf in the morning with Miss Cairns. You know fine that I always spend the whole of Saturday evening with you, watching the telly."

"Well, if you change your mind, or if your dear Miss Cairns can't play golf, you can go to the supermarket and get me a Bakewell tart."

"I'll ask the Gilchrist girl next door to get your Bakewell tart. And any other messages you may want; so you'd better get a list ready. I'm meeting Miss Cairns at nine-thirty sharp, and we're going to play at Muirfield this week. Miss Cairns says Muirfield's a much better course than Longniddry. Miss Cairns used to play at Muirfield quite a lot."

"Miss Cairns! Miss Cairns! It's never anything else but Miss Cairns," Mrs Hogg said. "I'm sick and tired of the sound of it. She's got another name, hasn't she? Why can't you say 'Mabel Cairns' and be done with it?"

"I always call her Miss Cairns. I never remember that her name is Mabel. She's always called Miss Cairns in the office."

"Well, for your information, my girl, it was Mabel Cairns when you went to school together."

"That's a long time ago. Times change, Mother. I don't remember much about my schooldays. Miss Cairns never mentions school."

"I suppose she's too busy talking about her golf handicap. What is it again? Not that I care a button. I disapprove of golf, as you well know. I disapprove of it for men as well as for women."

"But everybody plays golf, Mother. I don't see what you have against it."

"Well, for one thing, it keeps you on the links when you'd be better employed keeping me company and doing the shopping."

Alan Bold

TWO SCOTLANDS

1.

A solemn, bleak forbidding land of Nay
That saturates the soul with negatives.
A country where the lonely thing that lives
Is hatred, and it darkens every day.

Hear the low lamenting of the folk,
The open secret of the Scottish race;
Watch the features of the Scottish face
Harden as the Scottish people talk.

They gossip with the grimness of the lost,
Their guilt contains no massive mystery:
They stand condemned by ancient history,
Their dreams are haunted by a broken past.

The Scots confine themselves to thoughts of sin,
Culloden is the key that locks them in.

2.

Off wi' the molligrubs an' hoist your heid
For Scotland, you're no doutsum, you're no draig.
Your beauty shines from Yell to Yellowcraig,
You climp the hert, you blithely licht the gleed.

The flashy-fiery falls at Inversnaid,
The loch that louthers saftly at Menteith,
The Corrieshalloch Gorge, or duthe Dunbeath:
Sic places are the makin' o' the steid.

But mair than that, the ferkishin o' folk
Forgaither in a union o' faun sauls.
They shelf aa rabblach as they pack their awls,
The future is what maitters to the feck.

Scotland, rambust Scotland, caller licht
Is comin' in the gleen o' caller thocht.

Jim Kelman

As soon as I saw this photograph,
I thought: Yes, the same tee shirt,
I might've known.

Giles Gordon

She touched the rocking chair — bentwood curlicues, straw seat and back — and sat me in it. My room, my rocking chair. I knew about it, the chair.

— Go on, rock, she said; and smiled, encouraged me; as if it was a skill I had yet to acquire. — Rock as you usually do.

Ah, she understood that I'd done it before. Rocked on the rocking chair in my room. Or was she being tactful, sensitive to my anxiety about her instrument?

— As you usually do.

When thinking, creating, conjuring up worlds, words. Looking out of the window. Life passing, like a drooping, pouring hourglass, and my not noticing. The life I am rocking towards within my head.

— But I don't, I protested.

— Don't? What?

— Rock.

— You *must*, she said, surprised; as if to think, why then is the rocking chair there? as if everything, every possession in the room has a preordained, practical purpose. A rocking chair untenanted like an empty cradle. But if the baby has grown, grown up, learned to walk, walk away?

— You must, she said; and I sat back in it, rocked and drowned; and she clicked. The first click. I let out a sort of noise, a rasp, a little chortle. A sound.

She clicked again. And clicked.

— More coffee? I asked.

— No, she said. — Thank you. Shaking, shaking her head. She hadn't had any, preferring water, a glass. But most of it she hadn't drunk. Maybe coffee would have sent her to sleep, I'd no idea, none.

She'd come from one writer, was going to another. So many — well, three at least — Scots writers living in north London. Woo-ee!

— MacDiarmid won't be in the book, I said, and she looked at me, her eyes staring, startled, as if afraid, that I'd gone mad.

I meant: this will be the first time in years that a project of this kind, this book, will have been undertaken without his inclusion, thank God or Lenin. Which is not, not to say anything against the great erection, the blown-up thistle heid, only that another — MacLean, MacCaig? — will be the grand ancient man. Or woman.

— No, she said, looking puzzled, a little perplexed. — He's dead.

So, I thought, are others: Mackenzie, Gunn, Kennaway. And Spark's in Rome. And as my nervous, twitching, constipated face was taken — dark and light, heavy and bitter, very small beer — I was reduced, diminished, a tatter jock of the soul, drowning in my seat, bottom weighed down. And then my crown, my coronet. And then no clothes, no part to play, a writer having — once — written. Some words, thousands, hundreds of thousands even. To what purpose, point?

— Here are my children. This is Harriet, Gareth, Callum, the eldest. Photos of them on the wall by another photographer, years ago.

— Margaret, my wife. She had walked in, from shopping. Introductions. — Angela, she takes pictures. Catches our nobility for all time, in stasis. Rock, rock, the boat.

No. A shaking of the head, the black locks gone grey. The stoop, the paunch, the growing tiredness. The photographs stop nothing, certainly not the aging. Nor do they assist understanding, better writing.

And the boat went on bobbing, the rocking chair. Click. Click. The author caught, shot.

42

Liz Lochhead

WHAT THE POOL SAID, ON MIDSUMMER'S DAY

I've led you by my garrulous banks, babbling
on and on till — drunk on air
and sure it's only water talking —
you come at last to my silence.
Listen, I'm dark
and still and deep enough.
Even this hottest gonging sun
on this longest day
can't white me out.
What are you waiting for?
I lie here, inviting, winking you in.

The woman was easy.
Like to like, I called her, she came.
In no time I had her
out of herself, slipping on my water-stockings,
leaning into, being cupped and clasped
in my green glass bra.
But it's you I want, and you know it, man.
I watch you, stripped, knee-deep
in my shallows, telling yourself
that what makes you gasp
and balls your gut
is not my coldness but your own fear.

— Your reasonable fear,
what's true in me admits it.
(Though deeper, oh
older than any reason).
Yes, I could
drown you, you
could foul my depths, it's not
unheard of. What's fish
in me could make flesh of you,
my wet weeds against your thigh, it
could turn nasty.
I could have you
gulping fistfuls fighting yourself
back from me.

I get darker and darker, suck harder.
On-the-brink man, you
wish I'd flash and dazzle again.
You'd make a fetish of zazzing dragonflies?
You want I should zip myself up
with the kingfisher's flightpath, be beautiful?
I say no tricks.
I say just trust,
I'll soak through your skin and
slake your thirst.
I watch. You clench,
clench and come into me.

44

George Mackay Brown

THE SELLER OF OLD COATS

There was once a maker of stories and songs. He lived in an island. He hawked his stories and songs here and there. And up and down he went, here and there, in and out of magazines, and made profound utterances into microphones and tape recorders. He put together words that sounded fine and bell-like, or hushed and flower-like. He was quite pleased with himself, much of the time. But always at the back of his mind echoed the words of an old Border bard MacDiarmid to the effect that poetry wasn't of much account if it wasn't cherished in the fields and the factories. That is the ultimate test of the value of literature and of all the arts. *Coronation Street* and *The Sun* newspaper — those are what are discussed in the fields and the factories, the fishing boats and the supermarkets. Where will there ever be a singer to enchant the ears of the people until they turn away from *Coronation Street*? Where is the Pied Piper of the late 20th century, who will take us from the spoliation of the earth's resources (and wild sweet beauties) and the stock-piles of atomic death, and show us again Hesperides, Tir-Nan-Og, the Land of the Young?

Not this bard. What is the use of words, if they only add to the desert? So he opened instead a booth for the sale of second hand clothes. And along came a nice photographer called Angela from Glasgow and she took this picture of the old-clothes man waiting for a customer to show up.

Somhairle MacGill-Eain/ Sorley MacLean

AIR SGURR A' GHREADAIDH

Latha dhomh air Sgurr a' Ghreadaidh
Na mo sheasamh air an roinn àird eagaich,
Ag amharc sìos air Coire 'n Uaigneis
Troimh bhàrcadh a' cheò mun cuairt orm
Ann am bristeadh an t-siabain
Dhealraich aiteal òir air sgiathan
Iolaire dol seachad shìos ann
Ri taobh nam ballachan cliathaich;
Is dhomhsa thar glòir gach ianlaith
Aiteal òir an eòin Sgitheanaich.
Thionndaidh mi, 's a tuath 's an iarthuath
Bha Minginis 'na bòidhche shianta
Agus Bràcadal uaine;
Diùirinis is Tròndairnis bhuaipe.
Dhiùchd dhomh bòidhche an t-sàir Eilein,
Dhiùchd ,ach thàinig sian a' pheileir:
Ciamar a chumas an gaol seo
Greim air creig dheighe 'n t-saoghail?

ON SGURR A' GHREADAIDH

I was one day on Sgurr a' Ghreadaidh,
standing on the high notched knife-edge,
looking down on the Corrie of Solitude
through the mist surging around me,
in a breaking of the drift
a glimmer of gold shone on the wings
of an eagle passing down below
beside the flanking walls;
and to me above the glory of all birds
the golden glimmer of the Skye bird.
I turned; and north and north west
there was Minginis in her enchanted beauty,
and green Bracadale;
Diuirinis and Trondairnis beyond.
The beauty of the great Island rose before me,
it rose, but the bullet whizzed:
How will this love keep its hold
on the icy rock of the world?

Hector MacMillan

from his translation of *LE MISANTHROPE*
by Molière

PHILINTE   Man, whit is't? Whit's gaen wrang?

ALCESTE   Ah'll thank ye tae leave me.

PHILINTE   For aw that, Ah'll ask again. Whit like ...
bizarrerie....

ALCESTE   Let me be, Ah tell ye, and get oot o ma
sicht.

PHILINTE   Ye micht at least listen, withoot takin
licht.

ALCESTE   Ah *wull* tak licht, and wull not listen
mair.

PHILINTE   When yon wanease is on you, you vex
fowk sair; And though we be the best of
freens, Ah'm aye the first ...

ALCESTE   Me? Your freen? May Ah be curst!
Oh ay, till noo, you're richt, Ah hae
professed masel your freen,
But eftir whit, in you, Ah hae just seen,
Ah tell ye frankly, the kindness is
terminatit.
Ah need nae place in a hert that's ...
taintit.

PHILINTE   Ye've made up your mind then? Ah'm
tae blame?

ALCESTE   And wunner ye dinna dee o shame.
There can be nae excuse for whit you just
did,
And nae man o sense could be ither than
offendit.
Ah watch ye, near droon a man, wi a
flood o affection,
Pledgin yirsel his lifelang protection,
Embracin, wi promise, tae serve him
utterlie,
Smoorin him under a perfect spate o
butterie;
And then, when Ah spier wha he wis,
when he's gaen,
Ye scarce can tell me the bluidy man's
name!
Your great regard is greater still
evaporate,
The man means less than naething tae
ye, the meenit that ye separate.
— Great Goad! Whit gutless, vile
iniquitie,
Deliberately tae lower yinsel, t'betray
yin's ain integritie.
Gin e'er misfortune lured me tae sic a
wunner
Ah'd hing masel, instanter, in sheer self-
scunner!

PHILINTE   Ay weel, Ah cannae think th'offence
demands suspension,
Sae Ah'll tak leave tae beg your
condescencion
That Ah micht, wi mercy, temper a wee
your decrees,
And just refrain frae hingin masel — if
you please.

ALCESTE   This is scarce the time for pleasantrie.

PHILINTE   In earnest, then. What wad ye hae o me?

Nigel Tranter

from *KINGDOM COME*

Three men stood looking out of a window of the royal quarters of Stirling Castle, gazing down on the forecourt area, where there was considerable stir, dismounting from horses and shouting for grooms. Of the trio, one was in his mid-twenties and two of an age, in their forties. The young man was tall, red-headed, high-coloured and good-looking, and named James Stewart. But despite the fact that he was King of Scots, fifth of that name, and in the strongest fortress of his kingdom, he looked the least at ease, almost agitated, for one who was normally rather too carefree, not to say irresponsible, as a monarch, for some of his advisers. Of the two said advisers who were with him now, one was notably handsome in a smooth and almost delicate way, splendidly elegant, dressed all in scarlet; the other was much more rugged of feature and person but with a strong, plain face and keen eyes, plainly clad. They were respectively Davie Beaton, Abbot of Arbroath, Bishop of Mirepoix in France, Coadjutor and nephew of the Primate of Holy Church in Scotland and Lord Privy Seal of the realm; and Sir David Lindsay of the Mount, Lord Lyon King of Arms, Chief Usher to the King and Poet Laureate. These two eyed each other and their liege-lord significantly, as much as they considered what went on below.

"See you — you are to bide, both of you. Even though she bids you begone," James said. "I want you to be present. To note. And, and to support me. If necessary. She will be difficult, my mother. She, she always is. You ... understand?"

"Have no fear, Sire," Beaton told him, easily. "The situation is entirely clear, and all in your favour. We shall ..."

"Who speaks of fear, man? Sakes — I do not *hear* her! It is but ... awkward."

The other shrugged eloquent red-velvet shoulders.

Lindsay said nothing. Despite being the poet and playwright, the man of words, he was a deal less prompt of speech than was his friend.

Presently they heard voices from the stairway. Then, with the usual preliminary knocking, the door was thrown violently open so that it banged to the wall, and a woman swept in, followed by an over-dressed young man of almost beautiful appearance but looking distinctly unhappy, not to say dishevelled just then, hand out seeking to restrain her, members of the royal guard behind.

The lady, notably small eyes blazing, paused after a couple of paces into the chamber, then swinging round on the young man, who was in the act of making a hasty bow towards the King, actually pushed at his chest, thrusting him through the doorway with no little force, into the arms of the guard. Then she grabbed at the door again and slammed it shut in his face, before turning to confront the waiting trio.

"God's mercy — the insolence of that cub!" she exclaimed. "It is not to be borne. I will not be treated like some serving-wench — I, Margaret Tudor! The Queen. Do you hear? Dragged here by that fopling and his ruffians!"

"*I* sent Oliver Sinclair to bring you, Madam," James said. "I, I desire words with you."

"The more you are to blame then, James," she snapped back. She was a stocky, short woman of thick waist and middle years, sallow of complexion and unbeautiful, but with a very distinct presence and an inborn authority which by no means required her over-aggressive speech and manner to be effective. Dowdily-dressed, she was nevertheless overloaded with jewellery for horseback travel. But then, she was Henry the Eighth of England's sister ...

53

Trevor Royle

from *THE KITCHENER ENIGMA*

Many a young man caught dithering outside the recruiting office was encouraged to take the King's Shilling after contemplating Kitchener's exhortation, the call to arms which took a generation off to war. Yet Alfred Leete's famous recruiting poster is not the whole story: it, too, is full of contradictions. The face is clearly Kitchener's, but Kitchener's crudely depicted as a younger man — in 1914 he was sixty-four, greying, and heavy-featured. Even the eyes are wrong, beetling and too closely set together, although Leete was careful to give them a cold, arresting quality to increase the poster's impact. Only the moustache is Kitchener's, the instantly recognisable bristling hallmark of the stern warrior.

Any evaluation of the poster is bound to be unrewarding when it is compared to the photographs of the man himself. In his youth Kitchener was more than a little vain of his appearance and his photographic portraits show him to be a handsome, if somewhat reserved, young man. His eyes, piercingly blue and set far apart in a large face were especially noticed by his colleagues. 'His head was finely shaped, and the eyes, blue as ice, were in early life of singular beauty,' remembered his friend Lord Esher. 'Sandstorms and the Eastern sun ruined them in later years. Standing two inches over six feet, Kitchener was literally head and shoulders above most of his fellow men and he used his height to advantage to stare haughtily over the heads of those who stood before him. His large square frame, angular build and commanding presence set him apart from an early age, and in later life his face was made distinctive by its high colour, the 'sunburnt and almost purple cheeks and jowl' making a 'vivid manifestation upon the senses' of the young Winston Churchill when he met him in 1898 at the end of the Sudan campaign.

None of us can escape the legacy of our appearance. From his youngest years Kitchener's physical looks attracted much comment: he was considered to be almost too handsome for his own good in his youth, yet he allowed himself to become a prisoner to his moustache in later life. In the manner of the times Kitchener was invariably photographed looking fixedly ahead, seeing only what he wanted to see, oblivious to all distractions. The jaw is large and fleshy, the nose straight and elegant, the mouth cruel, yet there is a curious indecision and gentleness in the eyes. It is the face of a man who did not want to be forgotten.

Stewart Conn

AT THE HAIRDRESSERS

Behind white astragals, I sit
Waiting to have my hair cut.
Soon it flounces, a greying frazzle, about my feet.
The features in the mirror, sharply lit,
Resemble mine — but with more lines
Than I'd care to acknowledge — cut
Sharply in, as by theatrical make-up.

All round, women flit, as though part
Of a Japanese ritual; brown-smocked,
Hair rolled, silent as steam rises
And the heated water circles
Each dazzling sink. Resorting to no tricks
Of rejuvescence, I face facts;
Ask simply that it be trimmed, not too short.

On glass-topped tables Cosmopolitan and She,
All gloss, assist in the process
Of holding time, momentarily, at bay.
As the scissors snip, I am conscious
Of the plants in their pots, smooth leaves polished
On the surface — but each underside frayed,
Marking the tiny red spiders' unyielding progress.

Tom Leonard

*INTRODUCTION TO A DRAMATIC WORK
IN PROGRESS*

Once upon a time, there were three flying ducks on the wall of a Glasgow living-room. The living-room was papered in diagonal rows of pretty bunches of flowers, and the ducks were made of glazed china. The ducks flew permanently north-east above the bed-settee, between the door to the lobby, and the display-cabinet. The living-room, the ducks, the bed-settee, the display-cabinet — these all existed in the head of a small-time Glasgow writer, of semi-humorous and semi-*avant garde* habits.

It happened one day that this small-time writer was attending a run-of-the-mill sound-poetry festival in Amsterdam. He was sauntering down Eerste van der Heltstraat, turning a soundtext over in his head; being a semi-humorous fellow, he had a notion to present a spoof chamber piece that evening, which he was to call 'Beethoven's Ninth'; this he had allegedly scored for tenor, dead mouse, used contraceptive, bunch of grapes and banana.

He was having a quite chuckle to himself, when he was asked to share the source of his mirth by his companion that afternoon, an old Glasgow acquaintance who had taken up residence in the City of Tulips. This acquaintance was a tall, middle-aged fading hippie, who had drunk four bottles of Carlsberg Special and smoked two joints in honour of his friend's arrival. But when the small-time writer divulged his reasons for amusement, his irate companion upbraided him for being a wee petty-bourgeois wanker who had sold out to the London brigade, and biffed him on the side of the head.

Such was the force of this blow, that inside the writer's head, the ducks fell from the wall.

59

Tom Scott

from *THE DIRTY BUSINESS*

Let us remember
not only the Jewish men and women
remember
but suffer also the little children.

        In Rama
was there a voice heard,
lamentation and great mourning,
Rachel weeping for her children
and would not be comforted ...

Leah, with little Sol and Mischa,
taken in her time to the "showers",
petrified, ordered to hang up her rags,
hides the children among them, enters
the death chamber alone, praying
Boruch ato adonai elohaynu ...
Blessed art Thou, O Lord our God ...
But the SS search the clothing
and, too far to reach them,
she sees them pushed in and the door closed.

        In Rama
            Rachel weeping
                but in Dachau

Misery has outwept her tears.

Norman MacCaig

BY THE GRAVEYARD, LUSKENTYRE

From behind the wall death sends out messages
That all mean the same, that are easy to understand.

But who can interpret the blue-green waves
That never stop talking, shouting, wheedling?

Messages everywhere. Scholars, I plead with you,
Where are your dictionaries of the wind, the grasses?

Four larks are singing in a showering sprinkle
Their bright testaments: in a foreign language.

And always the beach is oghamed and cuneiformed
By knot and dunlin and countrydancing sandpipers.

— There's Donnie's lugsail. He's off to the lobsters.
The mast tilts to the north, the boat sails west.

A dictionary of him? Can you imagine it?
— A volume thick as the height of the Clisham,

A volume big as the whole of Harris,
A volume beyond the wit of scholars.

Donald Campbell

CAITHNESS GRANNIE

For Margaret C. Gunn

Far, far intil the North
amang the psalms and simple litanies
of a Sabbath country,
my Caithness Grannie watches
me critically,
takes in all
the faults and fancies,
follies and failures
I've managed to encounter
in the saga of my sair stravaiging
here in the sin-sapped South.

She need neither speak nor send
a word. Her watching eye
singles me out,
follows my fortunes,
fixes my presence continually.
I take care
to say my grace
to sup my broth in silence,
to clean my plate
and
mind my manners whatever I do.

John Bunyan leads me on
through the Slough of Despond.
Socrates stands speechless at my shoulder.

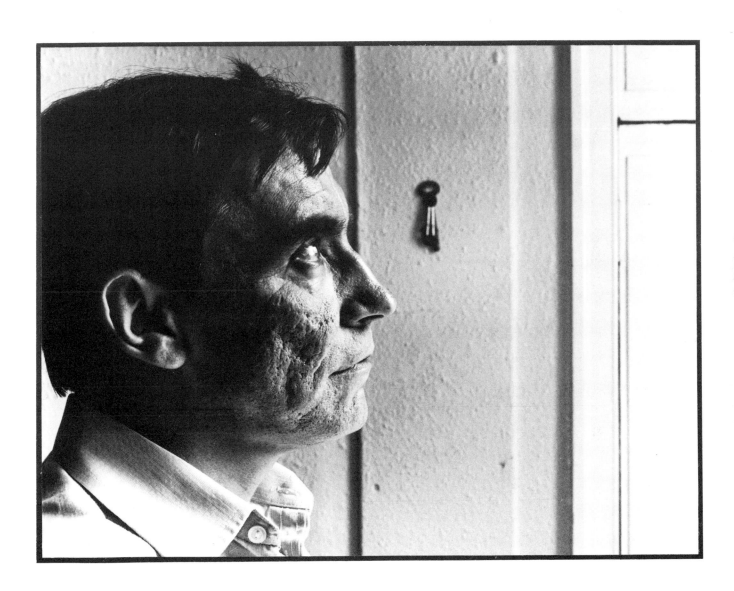

Ruaraidh MacThòmais/
Derick Thomson

Ma gheibh mi chaoidh a Ghlòir
(mar nach eil dùil agam)
'sann air sgiathan ceòl nan salm;
chuala mi 'n diugh, 'nam fhàsach,
preaseantair Leòdhasach air an rèidio,
's cha do dh'fhairich mi teas na gainmhich fo mo chasan:
bha riasg fionnar na mòintich fo mo bhonnan,
caora ag ionaltradh ann am poll,
's an oiteag a' gluasad a' chanaich.
Tha mi làn chreidsinn
gur h-e Leòdhasach a bhios anns an Naomh Peadair
ma liùgas mi steach air geata.

If I ever make it to Heaven
(not that I expect to)
it will be on the wings of psalm music;
today I heard, in my desert,
a Lewis precentor on the radio,
and I no longer felt the heat of the sand underfoot:
the exhilarating fibre of the moor was under my soles,
a sheep grazing in a bog,
and a light breeze stirring the cotton-grass.
I quite believe
that St. Peter will turn out to be a Lewisman
if I do sneak in at the Gate.

Naomi Mitchison

Anyone who has lived as long as I have must be aware of having been several people. Here are these old photos. Can I possibly be the same little girl standing in a sea pool wearing a big tammy and holding up an un-necessarily long cotton smock? No. And yet I remember the individual clefts in the big rocks round the pool, the sea anemones and all the life under the brown fronds of seaweed.

Was I the school girl with the long black stockings sitting up the tree? No, no, but yet I remember how one rushed out at the interval between classes to play tag or marbles or conkers for a packed five minutes between classes.

Perhaps I am beginning to be the young woman in the family photographs, part of the Haldane family but yet exploring outwards towards one of a dozen new countries of the mind. I was a wary teenager; most of my elders appeared to be intent on squashing me — not that, probably, they really were, only putting me in my place a bit. But how I loved people like dear Andrew Lang who seemed to believe me when I told him I was going to be a poet.

And the young wife? The gnawing of anxiety all the time during World War One? Yes, that was more or less me, incompetent at household affairs, always finding out from the latest book how I had gone wrong over baby-care or household management! I'm still rather incompetent, but it doesn't worry me any longer. I know I'm going to muddle through.

Then the time of writing, of living in two worlds, the wild excitement when my first book was published. There was a much smaller reading public then and a good review really started off a book. Nor was it only English language books; for several years I was reviewing recent French fiction for *Time and Tide* and knew what was going on across the Channel. Yet at that time I did not feel myself to be Scots rather than English, although no year went by without a family visit to Perthshire.

For five years I was writing *The Corn King and the Spring Queen*. When I began it I had little idea of what the people I had invented were going to do. While they were making up their minds I was writing stories or things quite unconnected with my main work. Later *The Blood of the Martyrs* overlapped a lot of politics. Another book which took a long time was *The Bull Calves* starting with much reading of eighteenth century Scottish texts. But by that time I had put down my adult roots in Scotland.

Yet most of my books were written after the war; I was then for some twenty years a County Councillor, member of the Highland Panel and later of the Highland and Island Advisory Council. I am surprised now to see how many different people I was, sometimes deep in Scottish affairs or turning to my other home in Botswana, sometimes back in ancient history, sometimes into science fiction. And when writing a children's book I had to do some re-living of my own childhood. Would I have done better to be only one person? Perhaps. Most of the really successful writers do one thing, remain one person. But it isn't so interesting for them — or maybe in the final judgment, their readers.

Maurice Lindsay

IMPROMPTU V: THOUGHT FOR THE DAY

Five hundred helpless foetuses a day
the woman said in her religious talk –
not soul stuff, but "The Value of Human Life" –
sucked out of careless womb to surgeon's tray.

What an absurdity when each same day
in jungles, ruined cities, ambushes,
dressed up to kill, men sally out of thought
to murder from, they hope, protective distance!

The world's too fully already. There's no room
for the unwanted. Praying doesn't pay:
and don't forget the young must have their fling,
believing that The Bomb's their destiny.

Some foetuses, she said, are heard to cry
before the silencing incinerator
puts paid to the mistakes they realised
but couldn't understand ...

                Switch the thing off!
What right have they to air such sloppy rubbish?
Has she forgotten all of us must die?
Abortion's just the basic throw-away
of our disposable society.

Ewan MacColl

from *THE SHIPMASTER*

DOBRA:

Ay, he's a hard-drivin' man, he is that! I only ever knew one other skipper that drove as hard as he does. That was wee Swanson, Tich Swanson they ca'd him, master o' a big limejuicer ca'd the *Kilmallie*. Do you mind the *Kilmallie*, Mick?

O'DWYER:

I do, I do, Dobra! If I remember right she'd a stump-t'gallant rig carrin' about an acre of canvas.

DOBRA:

That was her. You never got a minute's peace wi' that daft wee bugger. Get 'em up! Get 'em down! Day and night, night and day wi' wee Swanson hopping up and doon the poopdeck like a bantam cock. The particular time I mind, we'd left Falmouth on the same tide as a blue-nosed flyer ca'd the *Muskoka*. Her master was a bit of a Hellfire Jack ca'd Crowe.

O'DWYER:

I remember him well. A real Hell-or-Melbourne-in-thirty-days man!

DOBRA:

Well, Swanson was a wee bit jealous o' this Crowe character and he was dead set on beatin' him to Spencer's Gulf. There was a gale of wind blawin' up the Channel and Crowe decided to take the *Muskoka* up by the north o' Scotland where he'd hae mair sea-room. But no' Swanson. O dear, no! It's through the Channel and let her go! Well, we're managin' fine a' the way up until we're in the Trades and through the Trades and intae the Doldrums. My God! If you'd hae seen that man! There just had to be a breath o' wind, a whisper, and he'd hae us haulin' on the ropes, up in the shrouds or doon on the winches. Ye've seen they wee monkeys on sticks, well, we were like that; a day passed, twa days, three days, four, and Swanson's hoppin' aboot the ship like a blue-arsed baboon lookin' for bananas, only he's lookin' for wind. But there wasnae ony wind! So, do you know what he does? I'll tell ye what the wee mannikin does. he gets the mate to muster a' hands just before the dog-watch. All hands and the cook! And doesnae the cook dish oot an extra ration o' lime-juice to everybody aboard, officers included. Which would hae been fine if the stuff hadnae been primed wi' a load o' jollop. If you'd hae seen the way it worked on us! I'm no' exaggerating when I say the entire port-side was every shade o' broon by eight bells that nicht. It's a damned good job it rains a lot in the Doldrums so it was washed away before it had time to cake.

(There is a pause. Everyone is waiting expectantly for the point of the story.)

ROACH:

So what 'appened?

DOBRA:

That was just the first move in the master's wee ploy. At scaldgut time the next mornin', the cook serves up beans, as much as you could eat. For dinner, there's black-eyed peas, followed by bean stew and for a sweet there was powdered beans mixed wi' grease and molasses intae a kind o' dandifunk. It wasnae bad but, my God, before half-an-hour had passed ye began to feel that a typhoon was gaitherin' inside your bowels. And that was when Swanson's diabolical cunning came to the fore. He musters all hands again. Starboard watch behind the foremast, portwatch behind the mainmast, and the lazy gang, cook, carpenter, steward and midshipmen, behind the mizzen. At a blast frae the bosun's whistle, every man lowers his pants; at a second blast he bears his arse to the nearest canvas and then, following a long sharp blast, He breaks wind. Ay, ye can laugh, but it was no laughing matter at the time, I can tell ye. Thirty-eight men and laddies standin' there in the westerin' rays o' the sun fartin' awa' at fifteen-second intervals. For mair than an hour we kept that up, every man fartin' as if his life depended on it, and then that big lime-juicer begins to creak and groan. Then the mains begin to flap a wee bit and then ... she's movin'! I can tell you, a muckle great cheer gaed up frae thirty-eight voices while thirty-seven arses combined to unloose a fart that could hae been heard in Tierra del Fuego.

RILEY:

Why thirty-seven? What happened to the other one?

DOBRA:

Ah, I nearly forgot. The thirty-eighth belonged tae a Yank ca'd Muldoon. He had the squitters and he didnae want to chance beskitin' the skipper wi' a wild squirt.

(Laughter)

Elspeth Davie

I would say the camera has wonderfully sharpened the difference between private and public. This I think is a great merit in an age when this distinction is often blurred over. For in the pre-arranged photo, the camera — however gently and discreetly — is staring fixedly at a face or a figure and the person photographed is aware of what is happening whether he is posed at a table or lying in a field staring at a cow. That's to say, the cow still appears to be private, the man not so.

Above all the photographer has given us some wonderful crowd scenes — letting us know, for instance, what people feel about life in the huge modern city. Even so, there is usually one person who has suddenly caught sight of the hidden eye of the camera. Immediately an aura of awareness seems to surround him, he loses his flow of movement. Momentarily he freezes. He is said to be 'self conscious' This self consciousness is another matter and gets one into deep waters. I wouldn't go so far as to say the man staggers home wondering exactly what his self is, but he certainly knows there is more to it than the business of light and dark, black and white or dramatic expression and gesture. But all good photographers know this too and manage, rather miraculously I would say, to convey the feeling that their subjects have been looked at not only through a highly complex apparatus, but also through an understanding and human eye.

Finally I would say that writers — for all that they are supposed to have this so-called and greatly over-rated 'knowledge of human nature' — are not necessarily better equipped than any other persons for knowing themselves. Indeed they need all the help they can get. The camera may sometimes provide this.

Alasdair Gray

AUTOBIOGRAPHY

I am new born.
I want to suck sweet and sing
and eat and laugh and run and
fuck and feel secure and own my own home
and receive the recognition due to a man in my position
and not have nobody to care for me
and not be lonely
and die.

David Daiches

I write this furth of Scotland, rejoicing in the title of Distinguished Visiting Professor at the University of Delaware, U.S.A. Distinguished! Yeats, in a famous poem, once saw himself as 'a sixty year old smiling public man'. As I look, with some surprise, at this photograph of myself, I see myself as a seventy-two year old smiling public man. I suppose every writer is a public man in a sense: he has exposed himself by his writing, especially if he has, like myself, written a number of autobiographical volumes. Here at the University of Delaware one of the courses I am giving is on Scottish literature, and we have been reading Scott's *Waverley*. I asked the students how they saw the character of Baron Bradwardine. One of the girls in the class replied that she saw him as looking just like me. A gaunt military figure continually quoting Latin tags — I never thought of myself like that. I admit I quote Latin and Greek sometimes, in my old-fashioned way, but I am neither gaunt nor military.

Like the baron, however, I am old-fashioned, though in different ways. I was brought up on Hebrew, Latin and Greek (in that order), with a deep sense of European culture running through my veins and, as I grew older, seeing Scottish literature and history as very much a part of that culture. I fell into the academic life almost by accident: my interest in literature and in writing led me when young to believe I had a great career as a poet and novelist. It did not work out like that. Academic success led me into academia without any planning on my part, and I have always considered myself something of an oddity there. I have, for example, no 'special period', and in an age of academic specialists in literature (one is an eighteenth century man, or a Shakespearean, or a Victorian expert, and so on) I remain one of the last of the non-specialists. While writing my Oxford doctoral dissertation on Tudor Bible translation, I refreshed myself by writing a series of essays on the modern novel and modern poetry (I pride myself on being the first academic to write an extended critical essay on Joyce's *Ulysses*). Scottish literature and history have been another of my passionate interests, and my books on Burns, Scott, Stevenson, Bonnie Prince Charlie, the Union and Scotch Whisky testify to the variety of my Scottish studies.

Bridge-building is my vocation. My Jewish background, my Scottish upbringing, my literary passion, come together in odd ways. I once translated some of the poems of the Spanish-Jewish medieval poet Yehudah Halevi from Hebrew into Scots, a symbolic act, I suppose, though when I did it, as a young man, it seemed to me the most natural thing in the world to do. I can see rabbinical qualities in some of Henryson's fables. I know that today there is too much knowledge in the world for anybody to be able to master even a small proportion of it, and my old-fashioned combination of interests (even in the limited field of literature and history) is under continuous threat by dedicated experts on one man or one historical decade, or even, so help me, one poem. But never mind: one thinks and feels as one can and must, and for my part I have done so happily, and at seventy-two feel like carrying on as I always have.

Edwin Morgan

NORTH AFRICA

Why did the poets come to the desert?
They learned the meaning of an oasis,
the meaning of heat, fellahin's phrases,
tents behind the khamsin-blasted dannert.
We watched MacLean at the Ruweisat Ridge
giving a piercing look as he passed by
the fly-buzzed grey-faced dead;swivelled our eye
west through tank-strewn dune and strafed-out village
with Henderson; and Hay saw Bizerta
burn; Garioch was taken at Torbruk,
parched *Kriegsgefangener*, calm, reading *Shveik*;
Morgan ate sand, slept sand at El Ballah
while gangrened limbs dropped in the pail; Farouk
fed Fraser memorandums like a shrike.

Cliff Hanley

THE STORY OF MY FACE

It always bothered me slightly. When I was eight or nine, and being snapped in a family group, I always crossed my eyes so that the viewer would not imagine I took this bizarre object seriously. I still have these pictures, and apart from the skelly eyes there is nothing desperately wrong with the thing. More, it doesn't look at all like the one I **wear** now, it's quite a chubby little thing, a bit like Just William.

Earlier than that, though, it had worried me partly because I couldn't make out what it was *like*. Suddenly plunged into infant school, I became acquainted with the forty other brats, learned their names and faces and always got them properly matched because the Annie Enterkin face was unmistakably Annie Enterkin and a Johnny Preston face was certainly Johnny and nobody else.

But no amount of mirror-staring would reveal what a Clifford Hanley face was like, what category it was in. I once asked my mother what I looked like, and she said I looked quite nice, quite missing the point. She was a generous woman, and probably capable of hypocrisy too.

I got to know the bone structure in my teens, because I was constantly at the mirror again, doing self-portraits. (Contrary to widespread belief, I am not an extravert, but an introvert doing a very good performance.) They were back-to-front portraits, obviously, and they were determinedly posed, teeth clenched to create wee lumps of strength at the sides. But even my pencil couldn't add half-an-inch to the chin to make it tough. That is *not* why I grew a beard, though I did grow it to show off, because at that time, and it's over thirty years ago, nobody outside of a submarine or an art school had a beard and I reckoned the beard's time had come.

Now I know what kind of face I have. It's a face with a beard, and I sometimes get pretty bored with that too after all this time, but public pressure is on its retention. In general, I think I am reconciled to the face, but I don't stare at mirrors, and I don't burst into wild applause when I do, because I always have a razor in my hand, and whatever I think of the thing, I have no intention, now, of destroying it.

Joan Lingard

from *SISTERS BY RITE*

The old Volunteer was borne by his two sons and two nephews. They set off on the long haul to the cemetery at Dundonald. I mingled with the following crowd and went with them as far as Ballyhackamore where they put him into the hearse. I walked back with Mrs Robinson and she told me about some of the funerals she had seen. Women didn't go to the graveyard. They stayed at home to prepare the funeral feast.

And what a feast the McGills were making! Hams were on the boil on the old gas cooker, a large piece of beef was spluttering in the oven sending out a smell that made you feel daft for a taste of it, jellies were sitting on the window sills to cool, cakes of every colour lay on the big scrubbed kitchen table. There was no shortage of food in the McGills' house in spite of rationing. No dried eggs or liquid paraffin for them. They could get what they wanted on the black market which was thought fair game by everybody but my mother. A butcher who lived in the street made a fortune during the war selling chickens to American soldiers and shortly after VE day was able to move out to a big house up the Malone Road. They came back to visit from time to time in a long sleek black car, he with a fat cigar clamped between his newly gilded teeth, she wrapped in mink, with lips and nails tipped shocking pink. Granny McGill considered they'd gone above themselves and when they rang her bell she'd stand like a statue behind the lace curtains until they'd driven off. Even when they lived in the street she thought them vulgar with their tasselled blinds, mauve window surrounds and pink door with a plastic rose showing behind the glass panel. My mother always let them in, of course.

But on the night of the funeral the butcher and his wife jammed into the McGills' along with everybody else. Rosie and I sat astride the back of the settee. People squatted on the stairs and stood in the narrow hall. They ate and drank (ginger beer and lemonade — the McGills were strictly teetotal, which was one of the few things about them that my mother approved of) and sang. They sang the songs their fathers had sung. *Dolly's Brae, The Ould Orange Flute* and *The Sash*.

George Bruce

JANUARY VISITORS

We were visited by bull finches
this Monday morning. Immediately
we were in an exclusion zone: barriers
were set up: the chemical destructs
we had absorbed from laden airs
floated from us: the neuroses,
the nagging knowledge that our governors
were insane power seekers, the desperations,
vanished. Subtly these formal presences —
neat fitted black caps, deep-pink down chests —
persuaded us into their limbo.
Each green blade that pushed through snow,
each crumb set on the stone window sill,
presented itself in that new light of day.
(Yet through the pane the shadowed human face
that could not know that other place
where no time is, but every moment now.)
They sang no songs.
Doubtless they had no concern for us.
Doubtless they came for a meal.
Doubtless it was fortuitous they chose
our backyard for their landfall,
for that momentary enlightenment: gone
in a flirt of wings.

Jack House

AN ODE TO GLASGOW AUTHORS IN THE STYLE OF IMMORTAL BARD No. 2

(William McGonagall, Poet, Dundee, was born in Edinburgh but there is nothing in the Capital to commemorate that great occasion. His father, a weaver, moved to Glasgow, where the Bard received all the education he ever had — 18 months in a local school. The family flitted to Dundee and there he was visited by the Muse of Poetry and never looked back. Nevertheless, his favourite town was Glasgow and I have taken the liberty of trying to compose an ode in the Bard's style on some of the writers in Glasgow today.)

Oh, wonderful city of Glasgow with your triple expansion engines
In the building of which your workers get many singein's,
You are also famous for your writers, be it told,
And no doubt some of them are very clever and also bold,
Including Cliff Hanley who has made quite a name,
And is notable for being wee but game.
There is also Liz Lochhead, most beautiful to behold,
And Lavinia Derwent, whose books are still being sold.
On the subject of the ladies there is also Margaret Thomson Davis
And it would not surprise me if she whistles like a mavis
Because her books are selling well, which is also agreed
In the case of Alasdair Reid.
Then there is Edwin Morgan, poet, and him I do recall
In the Mitchell Library reciting his poems as loud as he could bawl.
Myrtle Simpson is an author who could write more, on the whole,
If she did not spend so much time at the North Pole.
I could mention more, like Maurice Lindsay, Alex Scott, Ronald Frame,
    Robert Crampsey and Jim Kelman
But to go into a list like that would need a bellman.
I end by saying all of them are a credit to Glasgow and the nation
And to name any more would be a work of supererogation.

Valerie Gillies

MRS GILLIES HER SONG

I'm not just a pretty word you know,
Baking my rough bread in the winter stove.
I can make out in the distance animals of light,
Hold conversation with the mountains by night,
Have words with the waterhorse, or speak
To pure things like the folded peaks.

Wearing frost bells on the backs of my hands
I gesture and step the thinking dance.
With an ivory whistle for my voice disguiser
My song will make you none the wiser.
Iron tongues with buzzing beads to hum
Rub spirit music on a talking drum;
Slit and strung nutshells on a rope
Make trappings for my harnessed antelope.

I rear green thistles beside dewy roads,
Small stars and young shoots in stackyards.
A stick for panther by the door is pinned,
My roof was whirled away by winds.
Stones and tributes enter my dream:
They come through the window where I lean.

Allan Massie

from *THE AUTOBIOGRAPHY OF THE EMPEROR AUGUSTUS*

It will not be dark tonight. Already, if I step out of my house, and look towards the east, I might see the Alban hills fringed with rose-touches of a new day. It is but two hours since we returned from the Field of Mars, and I cannot sleep. I sent the boy a moment ago to fetch me bread, and dunked a crust in the jar of wine from my own municipality of Velletri, and held it to my lips. The wine, poured a little early in anticipation that the ceremony would be over at the appointed hour, is already sharp with the faint musty tang of vinegar; it is always thin and yellow; yet I suck it from the bread gratefully.

Down in the plain, before the altar in the Field of Mars, with Agrippa by my side, I slit, with one sweep of the curved blade, the throat of a pregnant sow. I implored the blessing of Mother Earth on her children, the Roman People. The pig's blood spurted out — the sleeve of my toga stank of it so that I was glad when we came home to exchange the garment for this dressing-gown; then it trickled down the steps in the altar, and seeped through cracks in the marble to the imbibing earth. But there was one pool formed from an errant spurt that escaped the marble to the bare ground; the earth, parched by our long hot May, refused at first to receive it. It lay there in a viscous pool. I do not believe anyone noticed this but myself, and I am glad of that; they would be sure to see it as an evil omen, when it is only the slow working of nature.

I am tired and yet cannot sleep. I know the mood. It has come on me often, before great occasions, and I have learned to recognize it as an expression of divine intimations. Tomorrow is consecrated to Apollo and Diana — her chariot sails high above Tiber, I can see her light glint on the marble of the Forum which sleeps below; and very soon the Sun-God's rosy fingers will touch the Capitol beyond, and his own temple here on the Palatine; touch them with the new light I have given Rome. I say tomorrow, but it is already by some hours today, first of tomorrows. And there will be no blood in our sacrifices to Sun and Moon. The children will sing the new *Carmen Saeculare*, to bring these Games to full conclusion. I have instructed that every purpose of our four days' ritual be woven into the song: the first night's ancient ceremonies, with prayer an antique Latin which none now understands, then the recognition of our dependence on the bounty of Mother Earth, our prayers by day to the old tutelary Gods of Rome, and our welcome to the Gods of Light. I could have wished Virgil still alive to write the piece, for his spirit broods over these ceremonies which fulfil what he promised in his poem: 'Caesar Augustus, son of a god, who shall establish the age of gold in Latium over fields that once were Saturn's realm . . .' The bringing into light . . . I and Virgil. But Horace has done a commendable job; he has taste, if not vision.

I look to the east, as once, under the mountains of Illyria in a cold dawn of March, I gazed westwards . . .

Allan Campbell McLean

from *THE YEAR OF THE STRANGER*

I saw the soles of his feet first, naked as skinned rabbits, heels uppermost sticking out from under the ragged ends of his trousers. The timber from the keel of the old wreck had found water again; half of it was sunk in a pool under the quarry face. Mata lay under the timber, his head down in the water. I splashed into the pool, and got my hands under the curving wooden ribs that held his arms, and dragged him clear, pulling him over so that he lay on his back on the quarry floor. I got down on my knees, and took a hold of his face between my hands. His face was like ice. A shred of tobacco clung to his beard. I plucked it free, and it fell from my fingers into the pool. I watched the tobacco floating on the water for long enough before the tears came. Mata was dead. I had known that the moment I clapped eyes on his feet, but it was the sight of that shred of tobacco floating on the pool that brought the tears to my eyes.

I do not know how long I knelt beside him, weeping like a girl. Even when I was done weeping, I did not get up and go. It seemed wrong to leave him lying there, shackled fast to the timber, his arms spread wide to the cold moon. I thought to try to ease his hands through the staples until I saw the ridged flesh swollen against the irons. The staples had been hammered home until they were hard against his wrists. It would need a saw at the irons before Mata's body was rid of its burden, and the marks of the fetters on his wrists would still be there when they buried him.

I waited until a wisp of cloud had tangled the moon, and his face was in shadow before I got up and left him.

Domhnall MacAmhlaigh/
Donald MacAulay

DÀN AIR EILTHIREACHD......

Craobhan anns a' phàirc
a' dian-shileadh an dèidh an uisge
gaoth na sgal
fhathast gan criothnachadh
fras bhoinnean a' sprèadhadh
a earball na h-uspaig

ach an t-sìochain a' sgaoileadh
thar a' bhaile
a' ghaoth gheur sgaiteach
a' clothadh
a' ghrian a' dèanamh adhartais
'na sàthadh a mach a broinn na dùbhlachd

an fhuil eighreach ag aiteamh

òg-ghrian gheur sgaiteach
an earraich
ann an Obar Dheatha in
ri toirt uisg air mo shùilean

97

Sydney Tremayne

MOSES

Head in a cloud Moses stands
Beckoning with explosive hands
Threatening unpromised lands.

Tutmouse the Pharaoh rather bored
Hears the wind harp through his beard.
His heart is hardened by the Lord.

Superior persons tend to miss
Unreasoning people's deadliness.
Pharaoh is sunk because of this.

Pillar of cloud, pillar of fire,
Songs and timbrels fill the air.
Logic never led so far.

Moses harder than a stone
With the Laws engraved thereon
Knocks the gods and Pharaoh down.

In the desert furious,
Rules with God's and Pharaoh's voice,
For the chosen have no choice.

Aonghas MacNeacail

SAMHLA

sàth le d'léirsinn an sgàile, tha mise (sùil d'fhaileas) an seo
an clachan, an coire, an cochull do chridhe
mar phasgadh de shoillse reòit ann a linne céir

tha mi nam chidhis de dhathan, ach ged a bhiodh
eallaichean sùghar nan coille 'g abachadh nam ghruaidhe
am faic thu 'm madadh liath mireadh gu socair eadar na miaran

am faic thu portan is rodan a dannsa gu tiamhaidh fo'n chliabh
is nathair air spiris an ugainn, a deoghal do bhriathran gu'm fiaradh
agus siud, far nach robh dùil, air chùl chlaiginn, iolaire briathradh

gu'm bi an teist mar a bhà, cho cruaidh, cuairteach ri slige cnò
ach, ged nach brist mi tromh bhàrr mo ghréidhidh le sùrd
an tàmh tha mi luaineach, an tosd tha mi fuaimeach

APPEARANCE

pierce the veil with your vision, i (your shadow's eye) am present
in kirkton, in corrie, in the husk of your heart
like a folding of light in a pool of wax

i am a mask of colours, but even if
the succulent freight of the forest were ripening in my cheek
do you see the grey wolf quietly sporting between the fingers

do you see crab and rat dance solemnly under the rib-cage
the snake that roosts on the collar-bone, sucking your words to skew them
while there, unexpectedly, behind the skull, an eagle swears

that the proof will be, as always, hard, enclosing, shell of a nut
but, though i may not burst through the film that embalms me
in stillness i move, my silence gives voice

Mollie Hunter

from *I'LL GO MY OWN WAY*

It was the snow that began it all. "The cuckoo snow" they called it, because it was one of those late falls that can happen in April, when the cuckoo bird begins sending out its soft, insistent cry. But the two policemen on watch behind the hedge were unaware of this romantic notion, and of the part the cuckoo snow had played in the capture they hoped to make. The policemen had a thief in their sights.

The thief was a small, female figure. She had her back to them and she was kneeling beside one of a row of low, box-like structures — too far away from the policemen to let them see what she was actually doing there. But those structures were pens for breeding pheasants. And, the gamekeeper of the pheasant-breeding estate had complained, the pens were being robbed. Eggs were being taken from them, the eggs he should have had from the hen pheasants there. And what were the police going to do about that?

"We'll catch her," said one of the watching policemen, "red-handed!"

He was a big man with sergeant's stripes on his sleeve; and since kneeling in the snow did not come easily to him, his mood was not a pleasant one. The constable kneeling beside him was equally large, but being young and agile, his position was not causing him any great discomfort. More mildly than the sergeant had spoken, he asked:

"Who d'you think she is?"

"There's traveller families in the district — tinkers. And it's my guess she's from one of them."

Silently the constable acknowledged this to be a fair guess. All tinkers were thieves, after all — or so he had heard, at least. And who but a tinker child would be where this one was?

She was standing up now. She picked some objects out of the snow, bunched them into the front of her skirt, and moved off towards the road that ran along one side of the field. The policemen glanced at one another, then rose on unspoken agreement, and headed for their car.

Robert McLellan

from *ARRAN BURN*

Come nou to the muir's lost clachans.
See whaur the ash leans ower the lang shallas
And the gress is green by the forgotten ford.
Yonder dwalt folk that were sib to the fairies.
Adam their forebeir, watchin by nicht
Frae his wee stane hoose aneth his hillock,
Saw them won frae the stane ring by the men o the rude
And pey their siller penny to the viking
And their merk to the Norman, their sheepskin chief.

By their darg on this muir in their run rigs
They peyed their rent and held their banes thegither,
And nae disaster o wat, frost or drouth,
Nae blight or sickness in corn or beast,
Nae human epidemic or injustice,
Nor ony hazard o their baron's wars,
Sword or fire, or famine efter pillage,
Broke the lang line o their succession.

Yet they gaed in the end to make wey for sheep.

See the yowes graze nou wi nae man in sicht
And the breckans creep doun to the auld gortchens.
Seeds o thistles drift ower tummelt tintels
To sills and hearth-stanes on flairs o ling
In the grey ghaists o Gaelic byres and kitchens.
Through the tuin winnock hear the hish o the shallas
And the souch o the ash in the wind frae the balloch.

Wi the lambs and the whaups gane this is aa their elegy,
Though gulls may wail whiles ower some broken banes.

William Watson

from *THE KNIGHT ON THE BRIDGE*

Caesar cuddles his darling as if she were thistledown. Such closeness is a forgotten joy, and for each second of the embrace in which he holds it, he fears its end. He knows that when this meeting flies apart the cause will be that he has assumed too much, that he has held her too close, that he has forgotten he is a monster, mad and unforgiven. He fears at any moment to hear himself say something foolish, that will turn Bonne away. He holds back the wise and useful words he longs to speak, but which are sure to arrange themselves in meanings quite opposite to what he does mean.

How precarious, then, is this joyful moment! To Caesar it becomes a bubble which holds him and Bonne in perfect bliss, a bubble that any breeze may break or any whisper of his joints destroy. If he can keep still, if he can still his every nerve and silence his very mind, perhaps the moment will be enchanted into an aeon!

As things stand, however, Caesar has trouble sufficient unto the mere moment. He has been caught, when Bonne lays her bonnie bright head upon his chest, wrong-footed. He is, after all, inside the plum tree. Leaves tickle his nose. Broken twigs and the stems of picked plums are hazards to his eyes and vexations to his skin. In his ears rings the ominous song of a thousand intoxicated wasps, gorged but still guzzling on fermented fruit.

Meanwhile Bonne presses her face and her clenched fists against him, as a bad moment takes her. When it is past her hands loosen only a little and lie beside her pillowed head as if they are a child's, and she is one of those babes, already anxious in the cradle, who sleeps with infant fists curled tight.

It is from dilemmas like this that Caesar has been used to float up into thin air, letting the rough world get along without him: today he stands fast. He holds Bonne in his arms and keeps his feet on the ground, a prey to cramps, itches and the fear of sneezing such a sneeze that the bubble they are in will burst — this bubble which encloses them like the walls of a dream; from which the count of atrocities that tells the story of their love, is excluded; and where, with the quarrel of their two souls forgotten, they rest now heart on heart.

BIOGRAPHIES

David Black

David Black was born in South Africa in 1941 and educated in Tanzania and Scotland. His publications include: *With Decorum, The Educators, The Happy Crow* and *Gravitations*. He lives in London.

Alan Bold

Alan Bold was born in 1943 in Edinburgh where he attended university and trained as a journalist.

His *In This Corner: Selected Poems 1963–83* represents his best work over the past two decades; with the artist John Bellany he has collaborated on *A Celtic Quintet* and *Haven*. He has edited many anthologies including *The Penguin Book of Socialist Verse, The Martial Muse*, the *Cambridge Book of English Verse 1939–75, Making Love, The Bawdy Beautiful, Mounts of Venus, Drink To Me Only, The Poetry of Motion*. His most recent critical book is *MacDiarmid: The Terrible Crystal* and other works on MacDiarmid include his editions *The Thistle Rises: A MacDiarmid Anthology* and *The Letters of Hugh MacDiarmid*.

George Mackay Brown

George Mackay Brown was born in Orkney. Poet and story-teller, his latest books are *Time in a Red Coat* (novel), *Three Plays, Christmas Poems* and a story in a limited edition, with woodcuts by Charles Shearer, *The Hooded Fisherman*.

George Bruce

George Bruce was born in 1909 and brought up in Fraserburgh. The life of the sea-town was the main interest in his first collection of poems, *Sea Talk* (1944). At the time Bruce was a teacher in Dundee High School. His second collection, *Selected Poems*, was published while Bruce was a B.B.C. Producer in Aberdeen in 1947. By the time of the publication of his third book of verse, *Landscapes and Figures* in 1967, he was a Features Producer in Edinburgh. His *Collected Poems* was published after his retiral from the B.B.C. in 1970. From 1974 — 1980 he visited the United States as a Visiting Professor of English, including a spell in Arizona. In 1982 he was the Scottish-Australian Writing Fellow, and in 1984 he was awarded an O.B.E.

Ron Butlin

Ron Butlin was born in Edinburgh, where he now lives and works. He has published two collections of poetry, *Creatures Tamed by Cruelty* and *The Exquisite Instrument*.

Donald Campbell

Donald Campbell was born in Wick in 1940 but most of his life has been spent in Edinburgh where he has been a full-time writer since 1974. His poetry has been published in *Rhymes 'n Reasons* and *Murals*. Amongst his plays, written for the stage, radio and television, *The Widows of Clyth* was staged at the Traverse Theatre in 1979 and *Jekyll and Hyde* at Dundee Repertory Theatre in 1985.

Stewart Conn

Stewart Conn is a Senior Drama Producer for B.B.C. Radio. His first poems were collected in *Thunder in the Air* (1967) and *Stoats in the Sunlight* (1968) and his plays include *The Burning* (1972), *The Aquarium* (1976) and *I didn't always live here* (1976). His most recent collection of poetry is *Under the Ice* which was published in 1978. He was born in Glasgow in 1936 and now lives in Edinburgh.

David Daiches

David Daiches was born in 1912 and educated at George Watson's College, the University of Edinburgh and Balliol College Oxford where he did research on the English translations of the Hebrew Bible. He has taught at Chicago, Cornell and Cambridge and between 1961 and 1977 he was Professor of English and American Literature at the University of Sussex. His many academic studies cover a wide range of subjects, he has written on Robert Burns, whisky and the Scottish Enlightenment and in 1981 he edited *A Companion to Scottish Culture*. He lives in Edinburgh and his most recent book is *God and the Poets*.

Elspeth Davie

Elspeth Davie was born in Ayrshire and went to school in Edinburgh, studied at university and art college and taught painting for several years. She lived for a while in Ireland before returning to Scotland. She has published three novels: *Providings, Creating a Scene, Climbers on a Stair*, and three collections of short stories: *The Spark, The High Tide Talker, The Night of the Funny Hats*. She received Arts Council Awards in 1971 and 1977 and the Katherine Mansfield Short Story Prize in 1978. She is married and has one daughter.

Lavinia Derwent

Lavinia Derwent was born in the Borders but has spent most of her working life in Glasgow. She began writing for Children's Hour on B.B.C. radio and was the creator of 'Tammy Troot'. Amongst her many other books are the 'Macpherson' series and the 'Sula' books. For several years she was a prominent member of the committee of Scottish PEN.

Douglas Dunn

Douglas Dunn was born and brought up in Renfrewshire. He lived in Hull from 1966 to 1984 and now lives in Tayport. His most recent books of verse are *St Kilda's Parliament* (1981), which won the Hawthornden Prize, and *Elegies* (1985). His short stories were published as *Secret Villages* (1985), and he also writes plays for radio and television.

Dorothy Dunnett

Dorothy Dunnett was born in Dunfermline in 1923 and worked as a civil servant between 1940 and 1946. Her first novel, *The Game of Kings* was published in 1961 and introduced the adventures of a 16th century Scots mercenary, Francis Crawford of Lymond and Sevigny. Five further novels charted his Don Juanish wanderings in Europe: *Queen's Play*, *The Disorderly Knights*, *Pawn in Frankincense*, *The Ringed Castle* and *Checkmate*. She has also written a number of successful detective novels under the pseudonym 'Dorothy Halliday' and her most recent novel is *King Hereafter*. She is married to the author and former editor of *The Scotsman*, Alastair Dunnett.

James Allan Ford

Jim Ford, as he is known to his friends, was born in Auchtermuchty, Fife, and brought up in Edinburgh, where he was educated at the Royal High School and, inconclusively, the University. He served with the Royal Scots in Hong Kong and, after the surrender of the colony in December 1941, spent the rest of the war years in Japanese prison camps. His main peacetime career was a civil servant in, successively, the Ministry of Labour, the Inland Revenue, the Department of Agriculture for Scotland, the General Register Office for Scotland and the Scottish Office, from which he retired in 1979. His published work as a novelist consists of *The Brave White Flag* (1961), *Season of Escape* (1963), *A Statue for a Public Place* (1965), *A Judge of Men* (1968) and *The Mouth of Truth* (1972).

Valerie Gillies

Valerie Gillies was born in Edmonton, Canada in 1948 but her childhood was spent in Edinburgh. She was educated at the Universities of Edinburgh and Mysore in India and her first poems appeared in *Trio* in 1971 (with Roderick Watson and Paul Mills). A first complete collection *Each Bright Eye* appeared in 1977 and her most recent collection is *Bed of Stone*.

Giles Gordon

Giles Gordon, although born and brought up in Edinburgh, lives in London with his wife and three children. He works as a literary agent, and edits the British Theatre Association's magazine, *Drama*. He has published six novels, three collections of stories, and more pamphlets of poetry than he has energy to count. In 1982 his anthology with Fred Urquhart, *Modern Scottish Short Stories*, was brought out in paperback by Faber; and his *Modern Short Stories 1940–80* was published as an Everyman paperback.

Alasdair Gray

Alasdair Gray lives in Glasgow where he works as a writer and artist. His work include three novels, *Lanark 1982 Janine*, and *The Fall of Kelvin Walker*; and a collection of stories, *Unlikely Stories Mostly*.

Clifford Hanley

Clifford Hanley is something of a Scottish institution. His working life began in journalism, and branched into radio writing, the music hall, the legitimate theatre, song-writing and television. His first published book, *Dancing in the Streets*, an affectionate evocation of Glasgow childhood, was published in 1958, and in a score of novels and non-fiction works he has acquired a mass of happy readers. His thrillers under the pseudonym of Henry Calvin have a cult quality. Currently a popular radio and television performer, still a journalist, he has many more books to come, some serious but none of them solemn.

Hamish Henderson

Hamish Henderson has been a teacher and research worker at the School of Scottish Studies since 1951. He was born in 1919 in Blairgowrie and educated at Dulwich College and Downing College Cambridge; during World War II he served with the 51st Highland Division in North Africa and Italy. His collection of poems, *Elegies for the Dead in Cyrenaica*, published in 1948, has its origins in the North African desert campaign and was re-published in 1977. He played a leading part in the 20th century Scots folk lore revival and was responsible for the 'discovery' of Jeannie Robertson, the foremost ballad singer of modern times.

Archie Hind

Archie Hind lives and works in Glasgow, the city which forms the backcloth for his highly acclaimed novel *The Dear Green Place* which was published in 1966 and re-issued in 1984.

Jack House

Jack House was born in Glasgow in 1906, left school at fifteen to train as an accountant before 'seeing the light'. He trained as a newspaperman in 1928 and has worked on all three Glasgow evening newspapers. For twenty-two years he was a member of Scottish Round Britain Quiz team and he has appeared on countless radio and television programmes. He has written some forty guides to Glasgow and amongst his best known publications are: *Square Mile of Murder*, *The Heart of Glasgow* and *Portrait of the Clyde*.

Mollie Hunter

Author of 24 books for children and young adults. One book, *Talent Is Not Enough*, on writing for children. Has also published for adults, numerous plays, articles, essays. Subjects for children, fantasy, historical adventure, and realistic fiction. Has won numerous literary awards, including the Carnegie Medal, in 1975. Is much travelled as a lecturer on writing for children and has been twice Writer in Residence at Dalhousie University, Halifax, Canada. All but one of her books have a Scottish setting. Most recently published, *The Dragonfly Years* (young adult novel) and *The Knight of the Golden Plain* (fantasy). Born Longniddry, East Lothian, and has lived all her life in Scotland. Married. Two sons. Three grandchildren.

Robin Jenkins

Robin Jenkins was born at Cambuslang in Lanarkshire and educated at Hamilton Academy and the University of Glasgow. Between 1936 and his retirement he taught in schools in Scotland, Afghanistan, Spain and Borneo and these countries have provided the backcloths for much of his writing. His first novel *So Gaily Sings the Lark* was published in 1950 and his most recent book, a novel set at the time of the Disruption will appear in 1985. His short stories have been collected in *A Far Cry from Bowmore* (1973). He now divides his time between Spain and his home near Dunoon in Argyll.

James Kelman

James Kelman is a resident of Cumbernauld. His publications are: *Not Not While the Giro, The Busconductor Hines, A Chancer* and *Lean Tales* (with Alasdair Gray and Agnes Owens).

Tom Leonard

Born Glasgow 1944. Four areas of work: poetry in English and in a transcription of Glasgow dialect; sound-poetry, using tape-recorders; drama, especially satire — at present writing a play for the Traverse; criticism — also presently completing a critical biography of James Thomson (1834–82). His most recent collection of poetry is *Intimate Voices 1965–1983* which was published in 1984.

Maurice Lindsay

Maurice Lindsay was born in Glasgow in 1918, the son of an insurance manager. After training as a musician he served in the Cameronians during World War II and thereafter began a career as writer, broadcaster and journalist. In 1961 he became the first Programme Controller of Border Television; in 1967 he became Director of the Scottish Civic Trust and is now Honorary Secretary-General of Europa Nostra. He has written or edited more than sixty books, his most recent collections of poetry being *Collected Poems* (1979) and *A Net to Catch the Winds* (1981). He has also written extensively on Robert Burns and his *History of Scottish Literature* appeared in 1977.

Joan Lingard

Born in Edinburgh, brought up and went to school in Belfast. Author of nine novels and fifteen children's novels. Most recent novel is *Sisters by Rite* published by Hamish Hamilton in 1984. Children's books include the 'Sadie and Kevin' Ulster quintet and the 'Maggie' quartet which was adapted by the author in 18 parts for B.B.C. television.

Liz Lochhead

Liz Lochhead was born in Motherwell in 1947 and educated there and at Glasgow School of Art. She worked as an art teacher for eight years before becoming a full-time writer. Her first collection of poetry, *Memo for Spring* was published in 1972 and was followed by *Islands, The Grimm Sisters* and *Dreaming Frankenstein*. She has given readings and performances of her work all over Britain and she spent 1978–1979 in Canada as the Scottish holder of the Scottish-Canadian Writer's Fellowship. Amongst her work as a dramatist are *Blood and Ice*, performed at the Traverse Theatre, Edinburgh in 1982, *Sweet Nothings* for B.B.C. television in 1984 and *Dracula* for the Royal Lyceum Theatre in Edinburgh in 1985.

Donald MacAulay/Domhnall MacAmhlaigh

Born at Bernera, Lewis and educated at the Nicolson Institute and at the Universities of Aberdeen and Cambridge. He is currently Reader in Celtic at the University of Aberdeen. His poetry has been collected in *Seòbhrach ás a'Chlaich* (1967) and *Oighreached agus Gabhaltas* (1981) and he is the editor of the influential collection *Nua-bhàrdachd Ghàidhlig* which contains the work of his fellow Gaelic poets Sorley MacLean, Iain Crichton Smith, George Campbell Hay and Derick Thomson.

Norman MacCaig

Norman MacCaig was born in Edinburgh in 1910 and read classics at the University of Edinburgh. He has worked as a school teacher and was Reader in Poetry at the University of Stirling. He has published fifteen collections of verse, the most recent being *A World of Difference, The Equal Skies, Tree of Strings* and *Old Maps and New: Selected Poems*.

Ewan MacColl

Ewan MacColl was born in Auchterarder in 1915 and gained his first theatrical experience with the Glasgow Unity Theatre. For the Theatre Workshop he wrote the documentary ballad opera *Johnny Noble* in which traditional folk melodies are used for the linking narration. With his wife Peggy Seeger he has been closely associated with the revival of interest in British folk music and their *Travellers' Songs from England and Scotland* appeared in 1977. His most recent work includes *In Search of Political Theatre* (with Howard Goorney) and *Till Doomsday in the Afternoon* (with Peggy Seeger).

Somhairle MacGill-Eain/ Sorley MacLean

Sorley MacLean was born in Raasay in 1911, of a family of tradition-keepers, especially of Gaelic song. He had next to no English until he went to school, at the age of six. He got his secondary education at Portree High School and went to Edinburgh University (1929–33), after which he taught in Portree, Tobermory and Edinburgh, and latterly in Plockton in South West Ross. During the Second World War he was in Egypt and Libya, and was wounded three times, twice slightly but severely the third time. During the Sixties he greatly helped the late Donald Thomson and other teachers of Gaelic to save the teaching of Gaelic in Secondary schools and therefore in all schools. He was Writer in Residence at Edinburgh University 1973–75 and Resident Bard at Sabhal Mór Ostaig 1975–76. He has three Honorary Doctorates, and some of his poetry has been translated into French,

German, Dutch, Chinese, Italian and Welsh. He now lives in the Braes district of Skye, from which three of his grandparents came. He is married with three daughters and four grandsons.

Allan Campbell McLean

Born 1922, Walney Island, Barrow-in-Furness. Left school at fifteen. Fled Barrow-in-Furness at eighteen, courtesy of the Royal Air Force. Saw service in the Desert Air Force in Egypt, Libya, Tripolitania, Tunisia, Sicily and Italy, culminating in a court-martial for insubordination and 56 days imprisonment at Klagenfurt in Austria. Flown home, and married Margaret Elizabeth White on June 10, 1946. Three months later demobilised. Set up house with her as a freelance writer. The partnership goes on — from Kent to the Isle of Skye to Inverness.

Books published in the United Kingdom and Commonwealth, United States of America, the Netherlands, France, Portugal, Federal Republic of Germany.

The Hill of the Red Fox is the first of his children's books to appear as a Kelpie paperback.

Robert McLellan

Robert McLellan who died in 1985 was considered to be one of the greatest Scottish dramatists of the twentieth century. His first major play, *Jamie the Saxt*, was produced in Glasgow in 1937 and has been revived several times since then, most recently by the Scottish Theatre Company. Other work includes *Torwatletie* (1946), *The Flouers o' Edinburgh* (1947) and *Young Auchinleck* (1962). A master of the Scots tongue, he also wrote a series of 'Linmill' stories based on the rural Lanarkshire of his childhood as well as a long poem for television, *Arran Burn*, which was produced in 1965. From 1938 he lived at High Corrie on the Isle of Arran.

Hector MacMillan

Born Tollcross, Glasgow, 1929. Electronics engineer, mainly in research, till 1967. Freelance dramatist since then. Fair body of work for Radio and TV. Work for theatre includes: *The Resurrection of* *Matthew Clydesdale* (1971), *The Rising* (1973), *The Sash* (1973), *Royal Visit* (1974), *The Gay Gorbals* (1976), *Oh What a Lovely Peace!* (1977), *Eine Kleine Nachtmütze* (1981), *Capital Offence* (1981). Recent work includes: *Highest in the Forest* B.B.C. Radio 4 1982, *Out in the Open* S.T.V. 1983, *The Personal Touch* S.T.V. 1984. Violin making now developing into something more than a hobby as result of success at 1984 Facta Britannia Competition, in London, where a new viola was awarded certificate of distinction for tone.

Aonghas MacNeacail

Aonghas MacNeacail was born in Uig, Skye in 1942. He has acted as *Sgriobhadair* (writer in residence) at the Gaelic college at Sabhal Mòr Ostaig on Skye and also at Oban with An Comunn Gaidhealach. His work as a poet has taken on several reading tours to Ireland as part of an annual exchange of poets and musicians organised by the Scottish Arts Council and Comhdhail Náisiúnta Na Gaeilge and his most recent collection of verse, illustrated by Simon Fraser, *Sireadh Bhradain Sicir* was published in 1983.

Ruaraidh MacThòmais/ Derick Thomson

Ruaraidh MacThòmais was born in 1921 in Lewis. Since 1963 he has been Professor of Celtic at the University of Glasgow and he was the first recipient of the Ossian Prize in 1974. He has been editor of *Gairm* since 1952. His most recent publications are: *Creachadh na Clarsaich/Plundering the Harp* and *The Companion to Gaelic Scotland*.

Allan Massie

Allan Massie was born in 1938 and educated at Glenalmond and Trinity College, Cambridge. He taught for a number of years. Married with three children, he lives in the Borders amidst dogs, cat and horses. A journalist as well as author, he contributes regularly to *The Scotsman*, *The Glasgow Herald* and *The Field*. He has published four novels and four books of non-fiction. Novels: *Change & Decay In All Around I See* (1978). *The Last* *Peacock* (1980). *The Death of Men* (1981). *One Night in Winter* (1984). Non-Fiction: *Muriel Spark* (1979). *Ill-Met by Gaslight* (1980). *The Caesars* (1983). *Portrait of Scottish Rugby* (1984). As editor: *Edinburgh & the Borders in Verse* (1983).

Naomi Mitchison

Naomi Mitchison was born in Edinburgh in 1897. She is the daughter of the physiologist J.S. Haldane, sister of the biologist J.B.S. Haldane and she married G.R. (later Baron) Mitchison, an influential Labour M.P. She has written sixteen novels, seven collections of short stories and three dozen other books, many of them biographies and fantasies for younger children. Her best known novels are *The Corn King and the Spring Queen* (1931) and *The Bull Calves* (1947); and her most recent works are a collection of verse, *The Cleansing of the Knife* (1978), a collection of short stories *What Do You Think Yourself?* (1982) and a series of autobiographical studies.

Edwin Morgan

Edwin Morgan was born in Glasgow in 1920 and educated at Rutherglen Academy, Glasgow High School and the University of Glasgow. During World War II he served with the R.A.M.C. in the Middle East. Between 1947 and 1980 he taught at the University of Glasgow, being appointed titular professor in 1975. His *Poems of Thirty Years* was published in 1982 and amongst his many collections of verse are translations of Mayakovsky, Pasternak, Montale and Lorca. *Rites of Passage: Selected Translations* appeared in 1976. His most recent publication is *Sonnets from Scotland* (1984).

Walter Perrie

Walter Perrie was born in 1949 in the Lanarkshire mining village of Quarter. Educated locally and at Hamilton Academy, he took an M.A. in philosophy at the University of Edinburgh. Full-time poet and essayist, his last two volume-length poems have attracted considerable attention. The recipient of various literary prizes and awards, he lives in Edinburgh. His first collection of essays on the philosophy of literature — *Out of Conflict* — was published in 1982. In 1985 he lived in Vancouver as the Scottish holder of the Scottish-Canadian Writer's Fellowship.

Trevor Royle

Trevor Royle was born in Mysore, India, in 1945 and his childhood was spent in Malaya and Scotland. He was educated in St. Andrews and Aberdeen, and between 1971 and 1979 he was Literature Director of the Scottish Arts Council. A full-time writer, journalist and broadcaster, his previous books have ranged over football, military history and Scottish literature. His most recent publications are: *Death Before Dishonour: The True Story of Fighting Mac; James and Jim: A Biography of James Kennaway; The Macmillan Companion to Scottish Literature* and *The Kitchener Enigma*.

Alexander Scott

Alexander Scott was born in Aberdeen in 1920 and educated at the Central Secondary School, Aberdeen University and in the army, where he saw action as an officer in The Gordon Highlanders and was awarded the M.C. Since 1947 he has been a university teacher, retiring in 1983 as Head of the Department of Scottish Literature in the University of Glasgow. He has published seven collections of poems in English and Scots and is the author of many plays for stage and radio and of various features for radio and television.

Currently he is co-editor of the annual *New Writing Scotland* and he will shortly publish a third edition of the modern Scottish poetry anthology *Voices of Our Kind*.

Tom Scott

Tom Scott was born 1918 in Partrick, Glasgow, and as a result of the slump moved in 1931 to St. Andrews. Called up in 1939 he saw service in Nigeria from 1941 to 1943, then was posted to London where he stayed for ten years. In 1953 he went to Newbattle College under Edwin Muir and thence to Edinburgh University where he

took an M.A. and Ph.D. Since then he has given his time to writing poetry and prose in the service of Scottish literature, that most Sysiphian of labours.

The excerpt given here is from a poem of some 1200 lines on the Global War of 1939 to 1945.

Iain Crichton Smith

Iain Crichton Smith was born on the island of Lewis in 1928. He is a full-time writer, working in both Gaelic and English, and he has published novels, collections of short stories, poems and plays in both languages. His most recent publications in English are: *In the Middle* and *Selected Poems; The Hermit and Other Stories;* and *A Field Full of Folk.* His most recent Gaelic work is *An t- Aonaran.* He is married. *Mr Trill in Hades,* a collection of short stories was published in 1984.

Alan Spence

Alan Spence is aged thirty-five and was born and raised in Glasgow. He has published a collection of short stories, *Its Colours They Are Fine* (1977), and two books of poems, *ah!* (1975) and *Glasgow Zen* (1981). He has also had plays broadcast on television and performed on stage. He is completing a novel, *The Magic Flute,* and another collection of stories, *Sailmaker.* He and his wife run the Sri Chinmoy Meditation Centre in Edinburgh.

Nigel Tranter

Nigel Tranter was born in Glasgow in 1909 and educated there and at George Heriot's School in Edinburgh. During World War II he served with the R.A.S.C. and the Royal Artillery; thereafter he trained as an accountant before becoming a full-time writer. Between 1962 and 1966 he was President of Scottish PEN and between 1966 and 1972 he was President of the Society of Authors in Scotland. He is one of Scotland's most prolific writers with over one hundred books to his credit. His most recent books are *True Thomas* (1981), *The Patriot* (1982), *The Lord of the Isles* (1983) and *Unicorn Rampant* (1984). He lives at Aberlady and was awarded the O.B.E. in 1983.

Sydney Tremayne

Sydney Tremayne was born in Ayr. When he was sixteen he moved to Harrogate and after his father's business collapsed in the slump, he supported himself by working on newspapers in Yorkshire, Northampton, Sunderland and Newcastle. In 1938 he joined the *Daily Mirror* in London, where he became chief sub-editor, then leader writer. Later he was leader writer for the *Daily Herald.* He started writing verse when he was eleven and has had five books of verse published since 1948, the last of which, *The Turning Sky* (1969), received a Scottish Arts Council Award. He lives in Wester Ross.

Fred Urquhart

Fred Urquhart was born in Edinburgh in 1912, starting his career with publication of the now-celebrated novel *Time Will Knit* in 1938. Since then he has published three other novels and twelve collections of short stories and novellas. He has also edited a number of books, including *Modern Scottish Short Stories* (with Giles Gordon). Many critics consider him to be one of the finest Scottish short story writers of the 20th century. He won the Tom-Gallon Award for his story *The Ploughing Match,* and in 1984 he won the Barbara Campion Memorial Prize for his story *Kinderspiel,* which was published first in Switzerland in the multi-lingual periodical *2 Plus 2.* His most recent publications are *Palace of Green Days* (1979), *Proud Lady in a Cage* (1980), *A Diver in China Seas* (1980), *The Book of Horses* (1981) and *Seven Ghosts in Search* (1983).

William Watson

Novelist, playwright and journalist. Born in Edinburgh and lives in Glasgow. Sub-editor, *Glasgow Herald;* former literary editor, *Scotsman;* former literary adviser, Perth Theatre. Plays produced at Perth, Pitlochry, Traverse and King's Head Islington. Elected Fellow of Royal Society of Literature 1980. Scottish Arts Council visiting writer in Canada 1981–82. Novels: *Better Than One* (1969); *Beltran in Exile* (1979); *The Knight on the Bridge* (1982).